Photo of building

I0473442

Photo of tree

Photo of car

Photo of moss

Photo of kite

Photo of sailboat

Photo of bird

Photo of insect

_____

_____

_____

_____

_____

_____

_____

_____

_____

_____

_____

_____

_____

_____

_____

_____

Photo of river

Photo of sunset

Photo of clouds

Photo of a ball

Photo of rock

Photo of cat

Photo of dog

Photo of a vegetable

Photo of bottle

_____

_____

_____

_____

_____

_____

_____

_____

_____

_____

_____

_____

_____

_____

_____

_____

_____

Photo of dock

_____

_____

_____

_____

_____

_____

_____

_____

_____

_____

_____

_____

_____

_____

_____

_____

Photo of flower

Photo of lamp

_____

_____

_____

_____

_____

_____

_____

_____

_____

_____

_____

_____

_____

_____

Photo of horse

Photo of cow

Photo of hummingbird

Photo of full moon

Photo of leaf

_____

_____

_____

_____

_____

_____

_____

_____

_____

_____

_____

_____

_____

_____

_____

_____

Photo of lake

Photo of mountain

Photo of toy

Photo of shrub

_____

_____

_____

_____

_____

_____

_____

_____

_____

_____

_____

_____

_____

_____

_____

_____

_____

Photo of fruit